Josh's

The Official England Rugby

Annual 2009

Written by David Clayton

ENGLAND RUGBY

England

A Grange Publication

ISBN 978-1-906211-56-1

£6.99

Contents

Introduction

Welcome to the Official England Rugby Annual 2009! Packed with in-depth profiles on Danny Cipriani, Paul Sackey and Toby Flood as well as a special feature on the rising stars and new England Team Manager Martin Johnson, this annual should keep you busy during the times when there are no matches to watch. Plus there are stacks of exclusive features, quizzes, puzzles and posters that we hope you'll enjoy, while learning new facts along the way.

For instance, do you know which England star once had trials with Crystal Palace Football Club? You'll find the answer to that, as well as learning many more fascinating things about your heroes, in the following pages. Don't forget to have a pen and paper ready for The Big England Quiz – why not challenge a friend or family member to see who knows the most about the national team? But most of all have fun!

Martin Johnson -
Everything you need to know!

1970: Born in Solihull on 9th March. His first school was Welland Park School and he later attended Robert Smyth Upper School in Market Harborough

1987: Martin wins England Schools selection

1988: He joins Leicester Tigers Youth

1989: Martin gains England Colts honours and makes his senior Leicester Tigers debut

1990: Martin goes to New Zealand, playing for College Old Boys and King Country in the Inter Provincial Championship second division

1991: After impressing the New Zealand selectors, he is chosen for a two-week Colts tour of Australia, alongside such talents as Va'aiga Tuigamala, Blair Larsen and John Timu. On his return to England, he is selected for the England Under-21 squad, making his debut as a second row in a 94-0 win over Belgium

1992: Martin wins his first England B caps against France B and Italy B

1993: Martin makes his senior England debut against France at Twickenham after being called up as a late replacement for Wade Dooley. Has a steady game as England win 16-15. Later on in the year he plays final two tests against New Zealand after Dooley sustains a further injury

1994: Martin plays first full Five Nations campaign

1995: He enjoys Grand Slam glory, and is the only England forward to play throughout the six-match Rugby World Cup campaign in South Africa

1996: Wins his 25th cap during the Five Nations campaign, scoring his first try against Italy at Twickenham in November

1997: Named British & Irish Lions captain for South Africa tour, emulating previous second row forwards Willie John McBride and Bill Beaumont who led the Lions there in 1974 and 1980 respectively. The Lions win the first two tests to take the series 2-1 and Martin is appointed Leicester Tigers captain on his return

1998: Martin plays in all four Five Nations matches as England finish second behind France in the final table

1999: Appointed England captain by coach Clive Woodward, replacing Lawrence Dallaglio, and skippers his country to the quarter-finals of the World Cup.

2000: Misses the entire Six Nations campaign with an Achilles injury but returns in outstanding form as England draw series in South Africa. In November he captains England to successive wins over Australia, Argentina and South Africa

2001: Captains England for the Six Nations and leads his team to big wins against Wales, Italy, Scotland and France, increasing the winning run to eight matches and is later named as the Lions captain for the tour to Australia. He becomes the first player in history to captain the Lions on two different tours, though the Lions lose the series 2-1

2002: Leads his country for the 22nd time, overtaking Bill Beaumont as England's second most successful captain during a 45-11 victory over Ireland

2003: Leads England to a 42-6 victory over Ireland at Lansdowne Road to win the Six Nations Grand Slam and then skippers his

On 1st July 2008, England legend Martin Johnson became the new England Team Manager, heralding what is sure to be an exciting new era for the national team – here are Johnno's career highlights…

country to a 15-13 win against New Zealand in Wellington – the first English win in New Zealand for 30 years. There is further history written as England beat Australia 25-14 for a first-ever win on Aussie soil. Five months later he becomes the first England captain to lift a Rugby World Cup after a dramatic 20-17 victory over hosts Australia. He receives the CBE in the following year's New Year Honours List

2004: Retires from international rugby having played 84 times for his country, scoring 10 tries. He also made eight appearances for the Lions during a decade of fantastic service

2008: Named England Team Manager with effect from 1st July

RBS 6 Nations 2008

Weekend 1

England's hopes of continuing their Rugby World Cup form into the 2008 RBS 6 Nations campaign were dealt a severe blow for the opening game of the tournament after a second half collapse against Wales. Leading 19-6 with just 22 minutes left, England just needed to close the game out and play safe. There were no obvious signs that the Welsh were steeling themselves for a late flourish, but one misplaced pass opened the floodgates and Wales scored 20 points to win 26-19 and condemn England to their first opening day RBS 6 Nations defeat at Twickenham for 25 years.

Ireland beat Italy 16-11 and France hammered Scotland 26-7 at Murrayfield to leave Brian Ashton's side second-bottom in the table.

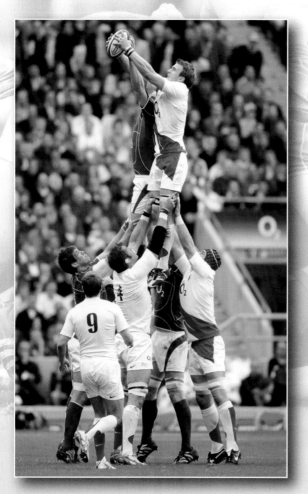

Weekend 2

A week later and England had to be on their mettle in the Rome sunshine where Italy were their next opponents. With Steve Borthwick at the helm deputising for the injured Phil Vickery, England turned around with a 6-20 lead. But the hosts rallied to within four points of England, who were relieved when they heard the final whistle. With a 19-23 victory on the board, there was at least something to build on, though France and Wales both recorded home victories on the same day to continue their battle at the top of the table.

Weekend 3

Now firm favourites to land the title, France knew they could end any lingering hopes England had of their first 6 Nations title since 2003. Eager to avenge their shock World Cup semi-final defeat, France were out of the blocks quickly, but Paul Sackey's fifth-minute try stunned the home crowd and a conversion and penalty by Jonny Wilkinson made it 10-0 with just 13 minutes gone. France were next to score a try which was successfully converted but Wilkinson scored a penalty within three minutes to make the score 13-7. A French penalty shortly after half-time and a drop kick and penalty by Wilkinson gave England the upper hand. Richard Wigglesworth's last minute try ensured a morale-boosting win for England, though Wales' 47-8 annihilation of Italy meant hopes of the title remained slim. Ireland's 34-13 defeat of Scotland left the Scots bottom of the table with two games to play.

Weekend 4

Only a victory in the Calcutta Cup would keep England's hopes of the title alive, but there would be no happier team in rugby if Scotland could extinguish their great rivals' hopes at Murrayfield – and that's exactly what happened. The hosts powered into a 15-3 lead with 48 minutes gone and though

England reduced the arrears to a try and conversion away from victory, Scotland deservedly hung on to win 15-9. France returned to winning ways with a 25-13 win over Italy, but, significantly, Wales won 16-12 away to Ireland, earning them the Triple Crown and edging towards the RBS 6 Nations title in the process.

Weekend 5

Going into the final weekend, only France and Wales could still be crowned RBS 6 Nations champions, dependent on various permutations and point margins. The best an unpredictable England side could hope for was to end a run of home defeats to Ireland and take the runner-up spot, yet with 10 minutes gone, the Irish led 10-0. However, tries from Sackey, Mathew Tait and Jamie Noon meant that England ran out 33-10 winners in a hugely entertaining encounter, most notable for a stunning performance from Danny Cipriani. Scotland returned to their pre-Calcutta Cup form by losing 23-20 to Italy and Wales completed a stunning 6 Nations campaign by thrashing France 29-12 at an ecstatic Millennium Stadium.

Final table:

	Pld	W	D	L	F	A	Pts
Wales	5	5	0	0	148	66	10
England	5	3	0	2	108	83	6
France	5	3	0	2	103	93	6
Ireland	5	2	0	3	93	99	4
Scotland	5	1	0	4	69	123	2
Italy	5	1	0	4	74	131	2

In Focus:
Mathew Tait

Tait was educated at Barnard Castle School, which has a reputation for producing promising young rugby stars - former England internationals Rob Andrew, Rory Underwood and his brother Tony all attended the school too.

Aged 16, Tait was capped for England Under-16s and later represented England Under-18s and Under-19s – all while he was still at school. He won a place at the Junior National Academy before being fast-tracked into the Senior National Academy in 2004. He joined Newcastle Falcons that same year, signing his first professional contract and scored a try against London Irish with his first touch of the ball!

Tait's star continued to rise when he was picked for the England Sevens and he was part of the team that won the Dubai Sevens at the end of 2004 – but the best was yet to come. One day before his 19th birthday, England coach Andy Robinson selected Tait for the senior squad's opening Six Nations match against Wales, making him the

second-youngest player to have appeared for England since World War II. Though he had a tough baptism and England lost 11-9, it was obvious that Tait was one for the future. Despite being dropped for the next game, he continued to impress, particularly for England Sevens. With them he helped his country to a silver medal at the 2006 Commonwealth Games in Melbourne, finishing as the tournament's top scorer with nine tries.

One of the stars of the 2007 Rugby World Cup, he almost scored one of the tries of the final in a mazy run but was stopped short. However, he wrote his name into the record books by becoming the youngest England player to appear in a World Cup final - at 21 years and 256 days.

He has also excelled in education and is taking a biomedical science degree, possibly with the intention of becoming a doctor after his playing career has ended.

At club level, he left Newcastle Falcons to join Sale Sharks in time for the 2008/09 season.

Mathew's younger brother Alex shows all the signs of following in his brother's footsteps and has already represented England at Under-20 level so it might not be too long before there are two Taits causing problems for England's opponents!

Described by former England star Mike Catt as "the future of English rugby", Tait is a fantastic role model for youngsters and will no doubt represent his country for many years to come.

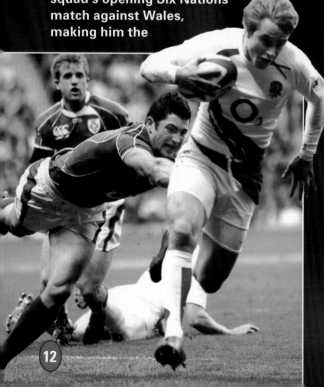

Mathew Tait is one of the rising stars of the England team. A versatile player, he can play centre, wing or full-back and apart from being an intelligent and creative player, he also has blistering pace that can tear opponents apart.

Spot the Difference?

Look at the pictures below, can you spot 8 differences between the two lineups? *(Answers on page 61)*

The Big England Rugby Quiz

1. Who is England's record points scorer?

2. Who did Rob Andrew succeed to become temporary England Team Manager for the 2008 Summer Tour of New Zealand?

3. Danny Cipriani was offered a contract by Reading Football Club. True or false?

4. What is England's nickname?

5. How many times have England appeared in the Rugby World Cup Final?

6. Who is England's record cap holder?

7. Which two countries have regularly competed in the Barclays Churchill Cup with England Saxons since its inception?

8. What is the capacity of Twickenham? A) 50,000 B) 72,000 C) 82,000

9. What is the Calcutta Cup?

10. Which nation did Topsy Ojo score two tries against on his England debut?

11. Which English club side did Martin Johnson spend his entire career with?

12. Where was Riki Flutey born?

13. Who beat England twice during the 2007 Rugby World Cup?

14. Which club does England winger Paul Sackey play for?

15. Who is England's record try scorer? A) Jason Leonard B) Rory Underwood C) Jonny Wilkinson

16. True or false: South Africa's Percy Montgomery was the leading try-scorer at the 2007 World Cup

17. England last won the RBS 6 Nations in 2003 – which two nations have shared the title for the last five years?

18. What are matches between England and France traditionally known as? A) Le Crunch B) The Battle of the Channel C) Le Clash

19. Who has won the Six Nations outright on 25 occasions? A) Wales B) France C) England

20. Which former England international took temporary charge of England's 2008 Summer Tour?

Dreams do come true!

Fun Stuff

Favourite food

Andrew Sheridan – fillet steak in a red wine sauce, with creamy mashed potatoes and vegetables followed by apple pie and custard

Toby Flood – meat!

Tom Palmer – pizza for starter then steak for main course

Jamie Noon – spaghetti bolognese

Mathew Tait – fillet steak

George Chuter – pizza

Peter Richards – pizza

Lewis Moody – shepherds pie

Josh Lewsey – good old-fashioned English grub, especially game

Matt Stevens – roasted macadamia nuts

Favourite music

Andrew Sheridan – These are the days of our lives by Queen

Toby Flood – Stadium Arcadium album by Red Hot Chilli Peppers

Tom Palmer – Arctic Monkeys

Jamie Noon – The Kooks

Mathew Tait – Coldplay – Yellow

George Chuter – Led Zeppelin

Lewis Moody – Foo Fighters

Matt Stevens – Counting Crows

Peter Richards – Pearl Jam and Metallica

Steve Borthwick – Killers, Snow Patrol or Nelly Furtado

If you weren't a rugby player, what would you be?

Andrew Sheridan – bricklayer

Toby Flood – student

Jamie Noon – school teacher

Mathew Tait – doctor, vet or dentist

George Chuter – a sheriff

Peter Richards – wine taster in the south of France

Josh Lewsey – an army officer, banker or farmer

Steve Borthwick – working in finance

Tom Croft – a property developer

Lee Mears – an RAF officer or working in the stock market

Luke Narraway – either at uni or helping with dad's butchery business

Simon Shaw –restaurateur

Olly Barkley - teacher

Nicknames

Andrew Sheridan – Sheri or Big Ted

Toby Flood – Floody

Tom Palmer – TP

Jamie Noon – Dowie or Noony

Mathew Tait – Taity

George Chuter – Big Nose

Lewis Moody – Moodos or Crazy Horse

Favourite joke

George Chuter: Q: Why was the sand wet?
A: Because the sea weed!

Practical joke

Josh Lewsey – I pulled down Steve Thompson's trousers once when he was being interviewed!

In Focus:
Paul Sackey

In his teenage years Paul was a good enough central midfielder to earn trials with Crystal Palace but he attended a school, John Fisher, in Purley, where rugby was the predominant game. He was spotted, as so many young players are, at the Rosslyn Park schools sevens tournament and an exciting career beckoned.

He first toured with the senior England squad in 2001, scoring two tries in the 82-21 victory over United States A.

Paul made his full England debut in November 2006 when he benefited from an injury to Mark Cueto to step in for the Twickenham South Stand opener against New Zealand and then scored a try in the next game against Argentina.

He has represented England U21s and Sevens and made his England A debut against Ireland at Northampton in 2002. He was selected for a third consecutive Barclays Churchill Cup in 2006 but had to withdraw with a toe injury. The following year he was part of the England Saxons team that defeated New Zealand Maori to win the 2007 Barclays Churchill Cup final.

In August 2000 he joined London Irish from Bedford and sandwiched two spells at the Exiles with a season at London Wasps (2003/04) before again joining the Men in Black in February 2005.

Injury prevented him joining England's summer tour of New Zealand, much to his disappointment, but the man who dreams of representing the British and Irish Lions believes he will return to action better and stronger than ever before.

"To miss two Test matches against the All

Growing up in London, Paul dreamed of wearing the three lions at Wembley rather than the red rose at Twickenham.

Blacks was a massive disappointment, even if the decision was taken out of my hands by experts worried that I would be risking long-term damage," said Sackey.

"I listened to the physios because I like to think I've got a few years left in me. I had a great season last year as a result of having a clear summer a year ago to rest, train and prepare. So hopefully being home again this summer will also have paid dividends.

"I want to be back in the England team for the autumn internationals and the RBS 6 Nations. I love being in the squad, I love playing for my country. But the British and Irish Lions is also a big motivation for me. In rugby, as in any other walk of life, you want to reach the top. You don't just want to be run of the mill. That means playing for the Lions."

Club: London Wasps

Position: Wing

Born: 08.11.79 | Westminster

Height: 1.83m (6' 0")

Weight: 91kg (14st 5lb)

Representative Honours: England U21s, Sevens, A, Saxons

Caps: 15

Points: 40 – 8T

International Record: 2006 NZ, Arg, 2007 F(1,2R), World Cup - SA, Sam, Tg, A, F, SA 2008 W, It, Fr, S, I

Four to Watch
in 2008/09

RIKI FLUTEY

Club: London Wasps
Position: Fly half/inside centre
Born: 10.02.80 | Wairarapa, New Zealand
Height: 1.80m
Weight: 89kgs
Former Clubs: London Irish, Hawke's Bay, Wellington, Wellington Hurricanes
Representative Honours: New Zealand U19, New Zealand U21, New Zealand Maori
International Record: Uncapped

New Zealand-born Riki Flutey qualified for England on the grounds of residency and England Team Manager Martin Johnson wasted no time in calling the London Wasps' playmaker into his first Elite Squad for the 2008/09 season. Prior to his inclusion in the England squad, Flutey, 28, said, "I spoke to family

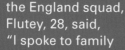

members and they were right behind me. The Guinness Premiership has enabled me to nail down one position instead of being a utility back and if the chance came to play for England, I'd grab it."

Riki Flutey joined Wasps in the summer of 2007 from London Irish. In his two seasons with the Exiles he scored an impressive 272 points, including 15 tries, in his 36 club appearances. Before moving to England, Flutey played for Super 14 outfit Wellington Hurricanes, as well as New Zealand Maori.

Riki started his career as a scrum half and it was in that position that he played most of his New Zealand age grade rugby, including winning the 1999 IRB U19 World Championship (an experience he lists as one of his best rugby moments). He switched to fly half whilst playing for New Zealand's U21s and in the six years since, he's moved between numbers 10, 12 and 15.

In 2007, he joined Wasps for "a new challenge," making his debut against Saracens that September. His versatility and ability to play all three positions saw him record 29 appearances and score 33 points in the 2007/08 season, including helping Wasps to retain the Heineken Cup and earning him the respect of his fellow players, who voted him PRA Computacenter Players' Player of the Year for 2008.

Outside rugby, Riki has a passion for music, singing, karaoke and playing the guitar; he hopes to play in a band. He also enjoys a wide range of sports including tennis, surfing and golf and he names his rugby hero as All Black centre Joe Stanley. He has an older brother called Mano, who has also played at every New Zealand age grade, and whom, Riki says, has had the biggest influence on his career.

JORDAN CRANE

Club: Leicester Tigers
Position: Number 8
Born: 03.06.86 | Bromsgrove, England
Height: 1.91m
Weight: 104kgs
School Attended: Colston's Collegiate & South Bromsgrove High School
Representative Honours: England U18 2003 and 2004 (captain), England U19s (2005 Six Nations, World Championship, captain), England U21s (2006 Six Nations and World Championship), England Saxons (2007 Six Nations v It, I; Barclays Churchill Cup v USA, S(R), NZ(R); 2008 Six Nations v I; 2008 Barclays Churchill Cup v USA, I, S)
International Record: Uncapped

The former Colston's Collegiate pupil, who lifted the 2005 Daily Mail Under-18s Cup, captained England U19s leading them through their most successful season ever, winning the 2005 Grand Slam.

Having stepped up to England U21s, he played in all five 2006 Six Nations matches en route to his second successive Grand Slam title and proved himself to be indispensable at club level, playing in 17 of Leeds Tykes' 22 Guinness Premiership matches in the 2005/06 season. He also captained the England U21 side that took on a Leicester Tigers XV in the Matt Hampson Challenge Match at Welford Road in 2005.

Now a Welford Road regular, Crane joined the Tigers from relegated Leeds Tykes at the start of the 2006/07 season, and has been likened by many Welford Road regulars to Tigers' great, Dean Richards, and returned the compliment by leading the team to a 31-13 victory over Ireland A in the squad's 2008 opener on home soil.

He was selected for the 2007 Six Nations England Saxons squad and made his debut against Italy A in February. Last year he was also part of the Barclays Churchill Cup winning England Saxons squad, playing in all three of England's games. In 2008 he was voted Most Valuable Player in the same tournament as England Saxons claimed their fourth title in six years.

Did you know?
A keen footballer, Jordan played for West Brom U13s and U14s and represented his County as an U16 and U18.

Four to Watch
in 2008/09

NICK KENNEDY

Club: London Irish
Position: Lock
Born: 19.08.81 | Southampton
Height: 2.0m (6' 7'')
Weight: 119kgs (18st 10lbs)
Representative Honours: Bucks U20s, South West, England Saxons (2006 Barclays Churchill Cup; 2007 Barclays Churchill Cup v USA; 2008 Six Nations v I, It)
International Record: Uncapped

Nick joined London Irish in 2001 at the age of 20 following considerable success as a basketball player at Portsmouth University from where he graduated in sports science.

He learned his rugby at Claire's Court School in Maidenhead where he played on the wing. Having moved into the scrum, Nick made his Exiles debut against Newcastle Falcons in November 2002.

An athletic forward, he quickly proved his class at London Irish and progressed to the professional squad, being named Young Player of the Season in 2002/03.

By the end of the last season he had made 103 appearances for London Irish, whom he helped reach the Heineken Cup semi-finals.

Nick was a member of the 2007 England Saxons squad for the Barclays Churchill Cup, playing against the USA in the opening game as well as in both the 'A' team Six Nations victories over Ireland and Italy that year. He also toured New Zealand in Summer 2008.

Did you know?
Nick's nickname is Kendo.

Last season Nick and Bob Casey consistently ranked as the most effective lineout stealing partnership in the Guinness Premiership.

Nick started his rugby career at Marlow RFC and attributes his success to the influence of Steve Williams, Ryan Strudwick and former London Irish coach Brendan Venter.

DYLAN HARTLEY

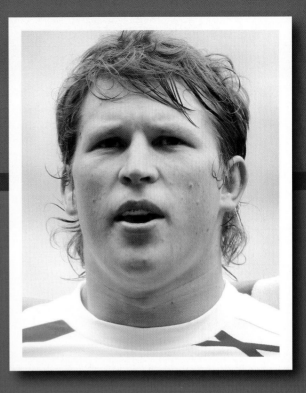

Club: Northampton Saints
Position: Hooker
Born: 24.03.87 | Rotorua, New Zealand
Height: 1.86m (6' 1'')
Weight: 100kgs (15st 11lb)
Representative Honours: England U18 Group Clubs 2003, England U19s (2004 Six Nations and World Championship, 2005 Six Nations and World Championship) England U21 (2005 Six Nations and World Championship, 2006 Six Nations), England Saxons (2007 Six Nations v It(R), I; 2008 Six Nations v I(R))
International Record: Uncapped.

Like Riki Flutey, Hartley chose England over the possibility of one day playing for the All Blacks.

Dylan was born in New Zealand, where he went to Rotorua Boys High and also played a few games for Bay of Plenty Under-18s.

He joined Worcester in 2003 after moving to England and was one of three players that joined the Northampton Saints Academy from Worcester Warriors at the start of the 2006/07 season.

After representing England as an 18-year-old (he qualifies through English ancestry) Dylan was selected for the U19 age group in 2004. After an impressive series of 2005 Six Nations and World Championship performances in his second year at prop for England U19s he was quickly drafted into the U21 squad for the equivalent tournament in Argentina later that same year, aged only 19, where he proved invaluable cover for all three front row positions.

In his first season with Northampton he quickly proved his worth, pulling on a Saints jersey on 16 occasions, often at No 2 with England hooker Steve Thompson adding his weight on the flank. His performances earned him a call up to the England Saxons squad for the 2007 Six Nations, when he went on to score a try in both matches against Italy A and Ireland A, before a disciplinary ban cut his season short and prevented his inclusion in the Saxons squad for the 2007 Barclays Churchill Cup.

After serving a six-month ban, the young hooker made an impressive return to action in National One last season under the tutelage of Dorian West, his former England U21 coach, helping the Saints win promotion back to the Premiership. He has been a key figure in Saints' undefeated promotion season, making 25 appearances and scoring five tries. He also toured New Zealand in Summer 2008.

Did you know?
Dylan's first stop in England was Crowborough in Sussex where he had an uncle and cousins of his own age. He joined the local rugby club and from there got involved with the England Under-18s set-up.

He has been working with Steve Peters, who has helped British cyclists Bradley Wiggins and Vicky Pembleton to conquer the world, to improve his performance.

In Focus:
Danny Cipriani

Seen as a future successor to England legend Jonny Wilkinson, Cipriani, who will be 21 on November 2, 2008, seemingly has the world at his feet. His path towards the top is an interesting one, with Danny's mother learning to become a London black cab driver in order to help fund his education and it was while he was at Donhead Prep College that his ability was first spotted, though he was something of an all-round sportsman, playing junior football for QPR and cricket for Berkshire and Oxfordshire.

"I had a chance to play sport every day," revealed Danny. "I played football, cricket, rugby, table tennis and squash. "I owe so much to my mum. She could have just worked normal hours and had a better life for herself. But she'd go out in the morning, come home to make my tea and then go out again in the evening."

It wasn't until he began playing for Rosslyn Park that his passion for rugby really kicked in and he was eventually signed by London Wasps, making his debut in 2007.

Possessing excellent pace, vision and kicking, Cipriani represented England at Under-19 level before being invited to take part in the senior squad's summer training camp, though he wasn't selected for the 2007 World Cup.

In May 2008 he suffered a serious ankle injury, ruling him out of the summer tour to New Zealand, though it is hoped he will have recovered in time for the 2009 RBS 6 Nations.

Club: London Wasps

Position: Fly half/full back

Born: 02.11.87 | Roehampton

Height: 1.84m (6')

Weight: 90kgs (14st 3lb)

Representative Honours: England U16s (captain), England U19 Sevens Commonwealth Youth Games Australia 2004, England U19s (2004/05 Six Nations and U19 World Championship; 2006 Six Nations and U19 World Championship), England Saxons (2007 Barclays Churchill Cup)

Caps: 3

Points: 18 - 4P, 3C

International Record: 2008 W(R), It(R), I

Danny Cipriani could possibly be the David Beckham of rugby union if he maintains his current rate of progress. The London Wasps fly-half made his debut against Ireland in 2008 amid much excitement from his ever-growing fan club of young fans and turned in a man-of-the-match display during a 33-10 RBS 6 Nations victory.

In Focus:
Steve Borthwick

Cumbria-born Borthwick is regarded as one of the game's best line-out technicians and analyses opposition line-out strategies studiously in order to gain advantage for his country. When he was handed the captaincy for the first time against Italy in February 2008, there was no prouder man around.

Borthwick has regularly led the England A team and won his first cap against France in 2001. He played occasionally over the next three years, but narrowly missed inclusion in the 2003 Rugby World Cup with his main rival for a place in the team, Ben Kay, getting the nod instead.

Borthwick continued to impress, however, and by the time the 2007 World Cup came around, he'd done enough to earn a place in Brian Ashton's England squad, though he was frustrated at only starting one game and coming on as a replacement on two occasions.

"There was a lot of frustration running through me during that tournament," said Borthwick. "I didn't feature as much as I'd planned, I felt I could have contributed much more than I did, and by the end, I saw it as a missed opportunity on a pretty significant scale."

"I wouldn't have been me had I not felt some anger. I'm fiercely committed to what I do and I'm very ambitious, so when things go badly, I take it to heart. That's my personality, and it's unlikely to change. But I dealt with that anger as I always deal with it: by analysing my performance, identifying the things I should have done better and resetting my goals."

Again, he channelled his energies into proving any doubters wrong and continued to play for his country whenever called

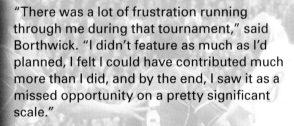

28

When England named their squad for the 2008 Summer Tour of New Zealand, lock Steve Borthwick was rewarded with the captaincy.

upon, so to lead his country for the first time against Italy in Rome was just reward for such a totally dedicated professional. He was one of only two England players to have played every minute of England's 6 Nations campaign in 2008.

At club level, Borthwick spent 10 years with Bath before joining Saracens at the end of the 2007/08 season.

The two tests he captained against the All-Blacks ended in heavy defeats and whether he maintains the armband or it returns to Phil Vickery will not be known until Martin Johnson, who included Borthwick in his first Elite Squad in July 2008, names his first team. Whatever the outcome, Borthwick will get on with it and continue to give his best for England every time he pulls the white jersey on.

Club: Saracens

Position: Lock

Born: 12.10.79 | Carlisle

Height: 1.98m (6'6")

Weight: 114kg (17st 13lb)

Representative Honours: England 18 Group, U19 Colts, U21s, A

Caps: 39

Points: 10 – 2T

International Record: 2001 F, C(1,2R), USA, Ro, 2003 A(R), W(2R), F(2) 2004 I, F(R) NZ(1R,2) A, C, SA, A 2005 W(R), It(R), S(R), Aus, NZ, Sam 2006 W, It, S, F, I, 2007 W, F(2), World Cup - SA(R), Sam(R), Tg 2008 W, It, Fr, S, I, NZ (1,2)

The History of the
Rugby World Cup

The winners would receive the William Webb Ellis Cup – so named after the Rugby School pupil who is believed to have first invented the game.

There was no qualification process for the first tournament as there were only seven member nations connected under the same governing umbrella and the remaining nine countries were invited. The All Blacks became the first world champions when they defeated France 29-9 in the final.

With the time between World Cups agreed at four years, England next hosted the tournament in 1991 with games played throughout the British Isles as well as Ireland and France and in a tense finale, Australia beat England 12-6 to claim their first World Cup.

Up until 1995 South Africa had not taken part in the World Cup due to an international sporting boycott, so when that was lifted, the Springboks were able to host the tournament under the watchful eye of President Nelson Mandela. With the South African public ecstatic to be once again involved on a global stage, the host nation capped a wonderful competition by beating the All Blacks in the final.

Wales hosted the 1999 World Cup and Australia claimed their second world title when they beat France in the final. With four tournaments completed, the motherland of rugby – England – had still not won the William Webb Ellis Cup and with the next competition once again to be held in the Southern Hemisphere, the chances of that run ending seemed slim.

Unlike the football version, which has been in existence for almost 80 years, the first Rugby World Cup only took place 21 years ago, with Australia and New Zealand co-hosting the inaugural event in 1987.

The 2003 World Cup would, however, provide the greatest day in England's history and finally bring the most coveted trophy in rugby to European soil for the very first time.

Though there were many favoured teams with more flair, Clive Woodward's England deservedly took their place in the final through a mixture of doggedness, grit and determination.

Claims that England were reliant on Jonny Wilkinson's penalty conversions and drop goals were, of course, untrue. This was a team of warriors led by captain Martin Johnson and each had a part to play. Wilkinson was a key member and his accuracy more often than not would edge tight games and the 2003 World Cup final proved to be just that. Deep into injury time, with the teams tied at 17-17, Wilkinson scored a breathtaking drop-goal just 26 seconds from time to win the match for England 20-17. A nation celebrated and close to a million people greeted the team on their return to London.

As the ageing team disbanded, England struggled to rekindle the magic formula that had made them world champions and as title-holders, they became a massive scalp for the opposition. Yet still, somehow, despite being written off and beaten 36-0 by South Africa during the 2007 World Cup in France, England dug deeper than ever before and slugged it out with a succession of teams, beating Australia and France to reach the final where South Africa awaited. It had been a monumental effort by Brian Ashton's team as they sought to become the first nation to retain the World Cup and ironically, they faced the team that had humiliated them earlier in the tournament – South Africa – in the final. Sadly, the Springboks – arguably the tournament's best side – just edged a close game 15-6.

Now Martin Johnson will aim to build a team capable of winning the title back when the 2011 World Cup is held in New Zealand. With Johnno in charge, you wouldn't bet against it, would you?

England v New Zealand
IRB Junior Championship Final 22/06/2008

The History of Twickenham
Happy Birthday Twickers!

Let's start at the beginning by asking how the idea of the stadium first came about? It seems that the RFU became convinced they needed a place to call their own as well as providing a permanent base for England following sell-out games against New Zealand and South Africa in 1905 and 1906, which had been held at Crystal Palace.

There was clearly a great appetite for the sport in England and it didn't make sense to play games in other people's backyards – why not have a brand new venue built instead?

Committee member William Williams was handed the task of finding a suitable plot to build a stadium and despite opposition from the locals, in 1907 a 10 ¼ acre market garden was purchased in Twickenham, soon to be nicknamed Billy Williams' Cabbage Patch! The land cost exactly £5,572 plus a few coppers and within a year, it had two covered stands housing 3,000 spectators each, plus a terrace at one end for 7,000 and an open mound at the other. The pitch was raised to avoid being flooded by the nearby River Crane and the total cost of building Twickenham came in at around £10,500.

in 1909, the stadium was ready for its inaugural game and Harlequins defeated Richmond 14-10. Satisfied the venue was capable of holding major games, three months later on 15th January 1910 England played their first ever game at Twickenham, beating Wales 11-6.

The home of the Rugby Football Union – Twickenham Stadium – is 100 years old in October 2009 and has hosted countless domestic cup finals and England internationals – but how much do you know about this famous old venue?

During World War I (1914-18), Twickenham was used to graze cattle, horses and sheep and for World War II (1940-45), the stadium was used as a Civil Defence Depot with the East Car Park dug up and used as allotments – not a million miles from how it had been before the RFU had purchased the land!

Over the years, stands were added, demolished and rebuilt as Twickenham grew in size and stature and today has a capacity of 82,000. In 1991 Twickers hosted its first World Cup final and today it is a magnificent international venue, hosting various domestic cup finals, RBS 6 Nations matches and The World Rugby Museum.

When England are firing on all cylinders and the capacity crowd is singing the anthemic 'Swing Low, Sweet Chariot', there is no finer place for any rugby fan in England to be – so happy 100th birthday Twickers!

In Focus:
Toby Flood

Born in Frimley in Surrey, but raised in Morpeth, Northumberland where he attended Chantry School, Toby was only six when he took his first steps towards stardom, turning out for his dad's junior side.

"My first memories are of being taken out of the house by my dad when I was a little kid because my Mum had had enough of me," says Toby. "I was shoved into Alnwick Under-8s aged six, the team my dad used to coach and I really enjoyed playing all the games that were associated with rugby, British Bulldog, that sort of thing, and also the physical nature of it all as I was a bit of a headless chicken when I was younger!"

Toby has this year established himself as a key player in England's midfield.

Claiming the No 12 jersey throughout the 2008 RBS 6 Nations, Flood recorded his team's first try of the tournament in the opening match against Wales, before adding another in the following game against Italy.

He replaced injured Newcastle Falcons team-mate Jamie Noon in the 2007 RWC squad, flying out two games into the tournament, and subsequently had a hand in England's progress to the final, coming on as a second-half replacement for Mike Catt against Australia, France and South Africa.

Educated at King's School, Tynemouth, Toby represented Northumberland Under 16s and 18s, was a county standard athlete and played cricket for the Under 16s. He appeared for England 18 Group and helped the Under 21s to achieve a second Grand Slam in three seasons in March 2006.

He played the first of his 17 tests to date off the bench for Charlie Hodgson against Argentina in November 2006. The following year he started England's RBS 6 Nations matches against France and Wales at No 10 and England's two summer tests against South Africa at No 12. Included in the 47-man Preliminary 2007 RWC training squad, he missed the final cut.

A product of the Newcastle Academy, Toby played for Alnwick and Morpeth before joining the Falcons in April 2003. He dropped a goal and kicked two penalties as a 19-year-old on his debut in the 29-28 win over London Wasps at Kingston Park in February 2005.

Did You Know?
Toby used to be a ball-boy for his beloved Newcastle United. He says: "It was towards the end of the season and we had to win and Manchester United had to lose. They won and went on to take the title. I never got to speak to Kevin Keegan or any of the players, but I did get one of Shaka Hislop's gloves. He brought a few out with him and I managed to get one, which is pretty cool. I think it is still back at my parents' house!"

Toby has a degree in Business Management degree from Northumbria University, he enjoys listening to the the Red Hot Chili Peppers and is a Newcastle United fan.

He and Falcons and England team-mate Jonny Wilkinson were born in the same Surrey town of Frimley.

Toby plays the guitar and is in a band with Newcastle Falcons team-mates Carl Hayman (rhythm guitar), Mark Wilkinson (drums), Jonny Wilkinson (lead guitar) and kit man John Stokoe.

It's amazing 23-year-old Toby Flood chose rugby ahead of acting considering his family background. Both of his grandfathers were actors – Gerald Flood featured in the television drama series 'The Ratcatchers' and Albert Lieven appeared in the film 'The Guns of Navarone'. His father, Tim, is the manager of Whitley Bay Playhouse.

Club: Newcastle Falcons

Position: Centre

Born: 08.08.85 | Frimley

Height: 1.88m (6'2")

Weight: 92kg (14st 6lb)

Representative Honours: England Students, Under 21s

Caps: 17

Points: 37 – 3T, 2C, 5PG, 1DG

International Record: 2006 Arg (R), SA (2R) 2007 S (R), It (R), F, W, SA (1,2), W(R), World Cup A(R), F(R), SA(R) 2008 W, It, Fr, S, I

Crossword

Figure out the clues, fill in the blanks and see if you can solve the crossword puzzle...

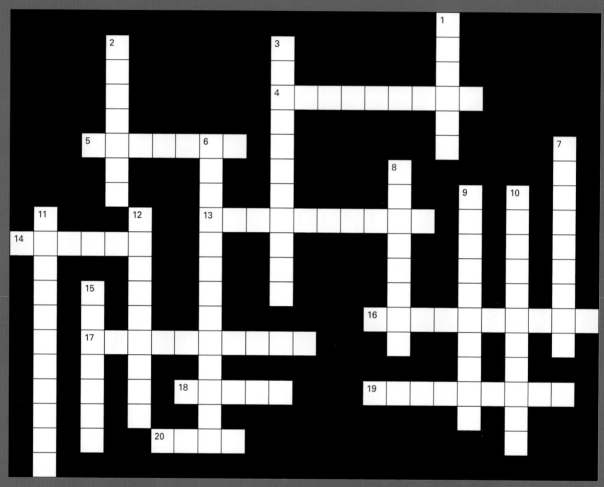

Across

4   He took temporary charge of England prior to Martin Johnson's arrival (3, 6)

5   Jonny Wilkinson did one of these to win the Rugby World Cup (4, 4)

13   Nickname for the South African team (10)

14   Nickname of England Team Manager (6)

16   The team Mathew Tait joined in 2008 (4, 6)

17   Destination for the 2011 World Cup (3, 7)

18   City where the 2007 World Cup final was held (5)

19   Nickname for the Australian team (9)

20   First name of Mathew Tait's younger brother (4)

Down

1   Name of England team that won silver medal at Commonwealth Games in 2006 (7)

2   You might take an early bath if you get _____ (4, 3)

3   Scotland's home venue (11)

6   Paul Sackey once had trials for this football club (7, 6)

7   Another name for New Zealand's team (3, 6)

8   This kind of tackle might bring you down with a bump! (5, 3)

9   Every England player hopes to be included in this (5, 5)

10   Current world champions (5, 5)

11   Paul Sackey's club side (6, 5)

12   Steve, who captained England's 2008 tour of New Zealand (9)

15   You need a helping hand to jump up for one of these (4, 3)

Crossword solution on page 61.

Wordsearch

How good are you at finding hidden words? You'll need all your skills to find and circle the 10 rugby-related words we've hidden in our wordsearch below. Remember, the words can be vertical, horizontal, backwards or diagonal...

N	T	N	N	L	R	E	T	H	H	N
T	X	P	Q	S	D	N	F	F	O	O
P	K	G	K	I	C	L	K	K	O	I
F	F	M	S	H	A	R	G	K	K	S
T	F	F	J	N	V	N	U	J	E	R
P	F	Y	K	P	Y	N	J	M	R	E
O	C	E	E	L	K	C	A	T	T	V
Y	R	K	R	E	F	E	R	E	E	N
L	D	P	E	N	A	L	T	Y	G	O
M	A	H	N	E	K	C	I	W	T	C
R	J	G	T	H	R	E	G	N	I	W

Conversion
Offside
Referee
Scrum
Hooker

Flanker
Tackle
Penalty
Winger
Twickenham

Answers on page 61.

Lionhearts

The British & Irish Lions have played under various names over the past 120 years – Great Britain, British Isles and The Home Nations. The combination of teams from England, Wales, Scotland and Ireland have been in existence since 1888. However, it wasn't until their 1950 tour of Australia and New Zealand that they adopted the nickname British Lions, due to the emblem on their jersey badges - though there was some objection from the people of Ireland who felt the name gave no recognition to their nation, hence the official name change in 2001 to The British & Irish Lions. Of course most rugby fans call the team The Lions regardless!

With a Head Coach selected from one of the four home nations, the team traditionally wear red jerseys and white shorts with blue socks and green trims – a representation of each member nation's flag. The strip was first worn during the 1930 tour of Australia and New Zealand.

Many players today regard playing for The Lions as a greater honour than representing their home nation and the tours, which take place every four years, have earned incredible interest both at home and in the Southern Hemisphere, where the matches are seen as epic battles by the finest warriors available on both sides of the world.

During the infamous 1974 tour of South Africa, the battle at the Boet Erasmus Stadium was one of the most violent clashes in the history of rugby – passions clearly run high when The Lions are in town!

Recent tours have seen mixed fortunes for The Lions. In 1997, Martin Johnson captained his side to a 2-1 triumph over South Africa – a first series win there since 1974 – but inspirational skipper Johnno couldn't prevent a 2-1 defeat to Australia on the next Lions tour, four years later.

In a break with tradition, in 2005, The Lions played their first ever 'home' fixture at the Millennium Stadium in Wales, drawing a match with Argentina. A comprehensive 3-0 test series defeat to New Zealand followed and the next tour in 2009 will see The Lions visiting current world champions South Africa, backed, as ever, by a noisy travelling army of fans from England, Scotland, Ireland and Wales.

Spot the Ball?

Answers on page 61.

Guess Who?

Answers on page 61.

England Saxons

The Saxons is the best place to see the next generation of England players in action. For the best players outside of the senior England squad, it helps them hone their skills and experience international rugby as they try to prove they have what it takes to make the step up to full Test honours.

After the launch of the Saxons side, former England Head Coach Andy Robinson said, "The future success of rugby in England depends, to a large extent, on the next best 15 players. The England Saxons will give up-and-coming players a place to perform in an international environment and to show that they can make the step up when required."

On July 1, 2008 England Team Manager Martin Johnson selected a 2008/09 England Saxons squad packed with exciting young guns like Nick Abendanon, Ryan Lamb, Anthony Allen who will learn the ropes alongside some more experienced pros like 2003 Rugby World Cup winners Joe Worsley, Mike Tindall and Ben Kay, who are hoping to force their way back into the senior side, and Danny Cipriani who is still recovering from a nasty ankle injury.

As well as nurturing the next generation of England players, the Saxons helps develop talented English coaches, like London

Irish coach Toby Booth and Newcastle Falcons' Steve Bates. Last spring, alongside experienced England coach Simon Hardy, Steve and former England prop Graham Rowntree guided the Saxons to victory against Ireland A and Italy A. In June, Graham, who only took up coaching after hanging up his boots in 2006, stepped up to work with the senior team making way for Toby Booth. Toby continued the good work as the coaching trio helped the Saxons lift the 2008 Barclays Churchill Cup in North America, beating the USA national side and Ireland A in the pool matches, before defeating Scotland A by 36-19 in the final at Toyota Park in Chicago, USA.

The outstanding players of 2008 included Harlequins flanker and skipper Will Skinner,

England Saxons is the stepping stone to the full international team. Formerly known as England A, the England Saxons name was christened in May 2006 and since then many of today's stars have passed through its ranks, including Danny Cipriani, Paul Sackey, James Haskell, Tom Rees, Tom Croft and Danny Care.

Gloucester Rugby duo Ryan Lamb and Jack Forster, London Irish scrum half Paul Hodgson, Leicester Tigers pair Jordan Crane and the 2007 World Cup finalist George Chuter, as well as Sale Shark Chris Jones, London Wasp George Skivington and Bath Rugby's deadly wing Matt Banahan. Matt's six tries in three matches helped him top the try scoring tables, while young Tigers' back rower Jordan was voted the Most Valuable Player of the Barclays Churchill Cup tournament, which England have now won four times in the six years since its inception.

The 2008/09 England Saxons squad is:

Forwards: Steffon Armitage (London Irish), Richard Blaze (Leicester Tigers), Louis Deacon (Leicester Tigers)*, Nick Easter (Harlequins)*, Jack Forster (Gloucester Rugby), Tom Guest (Harlequins), Jason Hobson (Bristol Rugby)*, Chris Jones (Sale Sharks)*, Ben Kay (Leicester Tigers)*, Michael Lipman (Bath Rugby)*, David Paice (London Irish)*, George Skivington (London Wasps), Andy Titterrell (Gloucester Rugby)*, Joe Ward (London Wasps), Dave Wilson (Newcastle Falcons), Nick Wood (Gloucester Rugby), Joe Worsley (London Wasps)*

Backs: Nick Abendanon (Bath Rugby)*, Anthony Allen (Gloucester Rugby)*, Matt Banahan (Bath Rugby), Mike Brown (Harlequins)*, Danny Cipriani (London Wasps)*, Ben Foden (Northampton Saints), Andy Goode (Leicester Tigers)*, Paul Hodgson (London Irish)*, Ryan Lamb (Gloucester Rugby), Ugo Monye (Harlequins), Topsy Ojo (London Irish)*, David Strettle (Harlequins)*, Mike Tindall (Gloucester Rugby)*, Dominic Waldouck (London Wasps), Richard Wigglesworth (Sale Sharks)*.

* Denotes players who have already been capped for England

Images courtesy of Jose Lagman

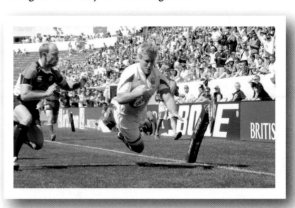

45

In Focus:
Topsy Ojo

Though not named in Martin Johnson's first Elite Squad, Ojo cannot have been far from the England Team Manager's mind and he is sure to return to challenge for a starting place again before too long.

Ojo was born on 28th July 1985 in Tottenham and though he spent three years with his family in the Nigerian capital of Lagos, the family returned to England when he was 10 when he attended Dartford Grammar School. He began playing rugby a year later and also excelled in athletics. He was spotted with his lightning pace and was soon called up to represent Kent and London & South East Schools at both Under-16 and Under-18 level, eventually joining London Irish's Academy in 2003.

Ojo, who reckons his best time for the 100m sprint is around 10.8 seconds, was soon playing for his country at various youth levels and played for England Under-18s, 19s and 21s as well as playing for Young England Sevens and England Saxons.

Able to play as either a full-back or wing, he made his club debut for London Irish in 2005 playing against Bristol, and has since become a huge crowd favourite. He spent time at the National Academy under future England manager Brian Ashton, who helped nurture Ojo's raw talent.

At 23, he is still developing physically, but he knows what he has to do to keep his strength up, although he is wary of adding too much power to his armoury in case it slows him down in any way. "I have built up muscle, but not so much that I have lost any speed," said Ojo.

"The extra work has helped me, especially when it comes to breaking the first tackle. Those half yards you make in contact are the extra step you need in order to get the off-load away."

That pace and power was evident against the All Blacks when Ojo provided the one silver-lining on a disappointing defeat. His first try was the result of an interception after which he ran virtually the entire length of the pitch to score a debut try and he added a second later in the game.

A good tackler, skilful and a player any opposing team would identify as a genuine threat, it's likely we'll hear more about the talented Ojo in the coming years at international level.

Club: London Irish

Position: Wing

Born: 28.07.85 | Tottenham

Height: 1.84m (6'0")

Weight: 83kgs (13st 2lb)

Caps: 2

Representative Honours: Kent U18 & Kent Schools (2001/02), London & SE U16 and U18, England U18s, England U19 (2001/02 and 2002/03 Six Nations & World Championship), Young England Sevens, England U21s (2006 Six Nations and IRB World Championship), England Saxons (2007 Barclays Churchill Cup v USA, 2008 Six Nations v It(R))

International Record: NZ (1,2)

Points: 10 – 2T

One of a collection of rising young English talent, Topsy Ojo has already shown what he can do at international level by scoring two blistering tries against the All Blacks on his senior England debut.

Hall of Fame

Martin Johnson
1993-2003
Position: Forward

An inspirational warrior, a leader and perhaps the greatest forward England has ever produced, Martin Johnson marauded rugby pitches at international level for a decade during which England enjoyed their greatest ever success. Johnno played 84 Tests for his country and after captaining The British and Irish Lions in 1997, he was given the skipper's armband for England in 1998, becoming the most successful captain in history. After captaining the Lions for a second time in 2001, Johnno's England completed an unforgettable double of a 6 Nations Grand Slam and won the Rugby World Cup in 2003. He retired from the international arena shortly after - at the very top. On 1st July 2008, he became England Team Manager and it's hard to imagine a better man to lead the nation towards a bright, new era.

Wavell Wakefield
1920-1927
Position: Backrow

Wavell Wakefield played 31 Tests for his country, 13 of them as captain. He played during three 5 Nations Grand Slams (1921, 1923 and 1924) and was knighted in 1944. In 1950 he became the RFU President.

Bill Beaumont
1975-1982
Position: Lock

Bill Beaumont played in 34 Tests for England and never gave anything less than total commitment each time he played for his country. He captained the side from 1978 until 1982 and inspired his troops to the Grand Slam in 1980 – the first time the feat had been achieved since 1957. He also captained the British Lions later that same year – the first Englishman to lead the side for 44 years.

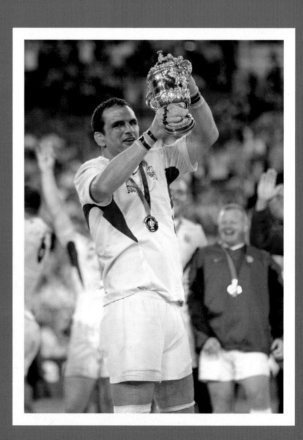

Some fantastic players have represented England over the years – here are six of the best…

Jason Leonard
1990-2004
Position: Prop
Jason Leonard's 14-year career as England Prop saw him amass a record 114 appearances for his country during a distinguished career – a world record until surpassed by Australia's George Gregan in 2005. He came on as substitute in the 2003 Rugby World Cup final and toured on three occasions with the British and Irish Lions.

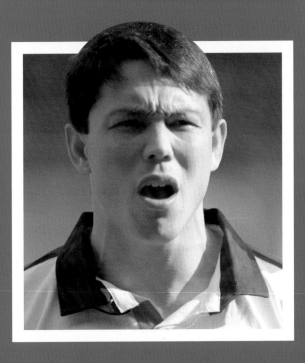

Jonny Wilkinson
1998-present
Position: Fly-half
One of the most popular players of modern times, points machine Jonny Wilkinson, OBE, has amassed an incredible total of 1032 in 70 matches for England. Only a succession of injuries has prevented both totals being far higher and he will forever be bought free drinks after scoring the drop goal that won England the 2003 Rugby World Cup. A vital member of England's all-conquering side of the late 1990s and early 2000s, Wilkinson's reliability and accuracy from penalties mean he has probably won more matches for his country than any other player and he is the record points scorer in both 6 Nations and World Cup history.

Rory Underwood
1984-1996
Position: Wing
Rory Underwood is one of England's greatest try-scorers having crossed the line on 49 occasions. Underwood played 85 times for his country over a period spanning 12 years during which time he played in three Rugby World Cups and represented the Lions on six occasions. The former RAF pilot was rewarded with an MBE for his services to England.

Sevens Up!

Because there are only seven players on the field, sevens matches are often fast paced, open and exciting. Playing sevens is an excellent springboard for younger players. It enables them to experience playing rugby on an international stage against world class opposition. Many of the England players of today have played sevens such as James Haskell and David Strettle and just recently we have seen the emergence of Tom Guest, Ben Foden, Matt Banahan and Danny Care to the England Saxons and senior teams.

England seasonally take part in the world's largest sevens tournament, the IRB Sevens World Series. The series contains eight legs, from which Dubai and Hong Kong are the fans' favourite with London, New Zealand and USA growing in popularity. England finished in fifth position in 2008 with New Zealand finishing top, followed by South Africa, Samoa and Fiji. England will also take part in the Dubai 2009 Rugby World Cup Sevens, which, like it's senior counterpart takes place every four years.

With the emphasis more on skill and speed, teams are, more often than not, comprised entirely of backs who are far more nimble and agile than the weightier forwards.

England's Danny Care celebrates scoring a try in the IRB Sevens World Series at Twickenham

The England Sevens team compete in various seven-a-side tournaments around the world.

It's not only eight players that are missing from sevens rugby, there are a number of other variations from the rules that govern senior matches. They are:

- Seven-minute halves, which are increased to ten-minute halves in championships.

- Five reserves are allowed, with only three interchanges.

- There is only one minute for half-time – increased to two minutes in championships, so not much time for the lads to get their breath back!

- Any matches that are drawn after regulation time are continued into Sudden Death Extra Time.

- Conversion attempts must be drop-kicked.

- Conversions must be taken within 40 seconds of scoring a try.

- Only three-man scrums are permitted.

- The scoring team kicks off.

- Yellow cards net a two minute suspension.

- Referees decide on advantage quickly.

- Additional officials such as goal touch judges participate.

Ben Gollings is England Sevens' world record points-scorer, bagging 1782 in total and scoring 158 tries. The team is coached by Ben Ryan who believes his team are shaping up nicely for the 2008/09 season. He said: "England can be a real force next season. In the next World Series and the World Cup in Dubai, England will hopefully be right up there at the top of the tree."

England Squad Profiles

STEVE BORTHWICK

Club: Saracens
Position: Lock
Born: 12.10.79
Birthplace: Carlisle
Height: 1.98m
Weight: 114kg
Caps: 39
Points: 10 – 2T

GEORGE CHUTER

Club: Leicester Tigers
Position: Hooker
Born: 09.07.76
Birthplace: Greenwich
Height: 1.80m
Weight: 101kg
Caps: 21
Points: 5 – 1T

JORDAN CRANE

Club: Leicester Tigers
Position: Number 8
Born: 03.06.86,
Birthplace: Bromsgrove
Height: 1.91m
Weight: 104kgs
Caps: 0
Points: 0

TOM CROFT

Club: Leicester Tigers
Position: Flanker
Born: 07.11.85
Birthplace: Basingstoke
Height: 1.96m
Weight: 106kgs
Caps: 4
Points: 0

England Senior Elite Player Squad 2008/09 (named July 1, 2008)

DYLAN HARTLEY

Club: Northampton Saints
Position: Prop/hooker
Born: 24.03.86
Birthplace: Rotorua, NZ
Height: 1.86m
Weight: 100kgs
Caps: 0
Points: 0

JAMES HASKELL

Club: London Wasps
Position: Flanker
Born: 02.04.85
Birthplace: Windsor
Weight: 110kg
Height: 1.93m
Caps: 8
Points: 0

NICK KENNEDY

Club: London Irish
Position: Lock
Born: 19.08.81
Birthplace: Southampton
Height: 2.0m
Weight: 119kgs
Caps: 0
Points: 0

LEE MEARS

Club: Bath Rugby
Position: Hooker
Born: 05.03.79
Birthplace: Torquay
Height: 1.76m
Weight: 100kg
Caps: 25
Points: 0

LEWIS MOODY MBE

Club: Leicester Tigers
Position: Flanker
Born: 12.06.78
Birthplace: Ascot
Height: 1.93m
Weight: 104kg
Caps: 53
Points: 45 – 9T

LUKE NARRAWAY

Club: Gloucester Rugby
Position: Number 8
Born: 07.09.83
Birthplace: Worcester
Height: 1.91m
Weight: 108kg
Caps: 5
Points: 0

TOM PALMER

Club: London Wasps
Position: Lock
Born: 27.3.79
Birthplace: Haringey
Height: 1.99m
Weight: 105kg
Caps: 10
Points: 0

TIM PAYNE

Club: London Wasps
Position: Prop
Born: 29.04.79
Birthplace: Swindon
Height: 1.85m
Weight: 119kg
Caps: 8
Points: 0

TOM REES

Club: London Wasps
Position: Flanker
Born: 11.09.84
Birthplace: London

Height: 1.84m
Weight: 98kg
Caps: 11
Points: 5 – 1T

SIMON SHAW MBE

Club: London Wasps
Position: Lock
Born: 01.01.73
Birthplace: Nairobi, Kenya

Height: 2.03m
Weight: 123kg
Caps: 48
Points: 10 – 2T

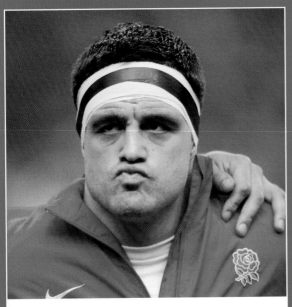

ANDREW SHERIDAN

Club: Sale Sharks
Position: Prop
Born: 01.11.79
Birthplace: Bromley

Height: 1.93m
Weight: 122kg
Caps: 25
Points: 0

MATT STEVENS

Club: Bath Rugby
Position: Prop
Born: 01.10.82
Birthplace: Durban, South Africa

Height: 1.87m
Weight: 121kg
Caps: 28
Points: 0

England Squad Profiles

PHIL VICKERY MBE

Club: London Wasps
Position: Prop
Born: 14.03.76
Birthplace: Barnstaple

Height: 1.90m
Weight: 120kg
Caps: 64
Points: 10 – 2T

OLLY BARKLEY

Club: Gloucester Rugby
Position: Fly half
Born: 28.11.81
Birthplace: Hammersmith

Height: 1.80m
Weight: 92kg
Caps: 23
Points: 82 – 2T, 9C, 18P

DANNY CARE

Club: Harlequins
Position: Scrum half
Born: 02.01.87
Birthplace: Leeds

Height: 1.75m
Weight: 76kg
Caps: 2
Points: 5 – 1T

HARRY ELLIS

Club: Leicester Tigers
Position: Scrum half
Born: 17.05.82
Birthplace: Wigston

Height: 1.78m
Weight: 86kg
Caps: 13
Points: 15 – 3T

TOBY FLOOD

Club: Leicester Tigers
Position: Centre
Born: 08.08.85
Birthplace: Frimley, Surrey

Height: 1.88m
Weight: 92kg
Caps: 18
Points: 37 – 3T, 2C, 5P, 1DG

RIKI FLUTEY

Club: London Wasps
Position: Centre
Born: 10.02.80
Birthplace: Wairarapa, NZ

Height: 1.78m
Weight: 88kgs
Caps: 0
Points: 0

SHANE GERAGHTY

Club: London Irish
Position: Fly half/centre
Born: 12.08.86
Birthplace: Coventry

Height: 1.80m
Weight: 83kg
Caps: 2
Points: 5 – 1C, 1P

DAN HIPKISS

Club: Leicester Tigers
Position: Centre
Born: 04.06.82
Birthplace: Ipswich

Height: 1.79m
Weight: 92 kg
Caps: 6
Points: 0

JOSH LEWSEY MBE

Club: London Wasps
Position: Wing/ full back
Born: 30.11.76
Birthplace: Bromley
Height: 1.80m
Weight: 88kg
Caps: 55
Points: 110 – 22T

JAMIE NOON

Club: Newcastle Falcons
Position: Centre
Born: 09.05.79
Birthplace: Goole
Height: 1.78m
Weight: 89kg
Caps: 33
Points: 35 – 7T

PETER RICHARDS

Club: London Irish
Position: Scrum half
Born: 10.03.78
Birthplace: Portsmouth
Height: 1.77m
Weight: 87kg
Caps: 12
Points: 0

PAUL SACKEY

Club: London Wasps
Position: Wing
Born: 08.11.79
Birthplace: Westminster
Height: 1.83m
Weight: 91kg
Caps: 15
Points: 40 – 8T

JAMES SIMPSON-DANIEL

Club: Gloucester Rugby
Position: Centre/wing
Born: 30.5.82
Birthplace: Stockton-on-Tees

Height: 1.82m
Weight: 79kg
Caps: 10
Points: 15 – 3T

MATHEW TAIT

Club: Sale Sharks
Position: Centre
Born: 06.02.86
Birthplace: Shotley Bridge

Height: 1.83m
Weight: 90kg
Caps: 24
Points: 15 – 3T

TOM VARNDELL

Club: Leicester Tigers
Position: Wing
Born: 16.09.85,
Birthplace: Ashford, Kent

Height: 1.92m
Weight: 97kg
Caps: 4
Points: 15 – 3T

JONNY WILKINSON OBE

Club: Newcastle Falcons
Position: Fly half
Born: 25.05.79
Birthplace: Frimley

Height: 1.77m
Weight: 88kg
Caps: 70
Points: 1032 – 6T, 144C, 209P, 29DG

Quiz Answers

Spot the Difference (p.15)

Wordsearch (p.39)

N	T	N	N	L	R	E	T	H	H	N
T	X	P	Q	S	D	N	F	F	O	O
P	K	G	K	I	C	L	K	K	O	I
F	F	M	S	H	A	R	G	K	K	S
T	F	F	J	N	V	N	U	J	E	R
P	F	Y	K	P	Y	N	J	M	R	E
O	C	E	E	L	K	C	A	T	T	V
Y	R	K	R	E	F	E	R	E	E	N
L	D	P	E	N	A	L	T	Y	G	O
M	A	H	N	E	K	C	I	W	T	C
R	J	G	T	H	R	E	G	N	I	W

Spot the Ball? (p.41)

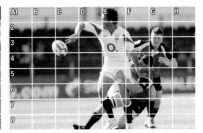

Big Quiz (p.16)
1.   Johnny Wilkinson
2.   Brian Ashton
3.   True
4.   The Red and Whites
5.   Three – in 1991, 2003 and 2007
6.   Jason Leonard (114 caps)
7.   USA & Canada
8.   C) 82,000
9.   An annual Six Nations clash between England and Scotland
10. New Zealand
11. Leicester Tigers (1989-2005)
12. New Zealand
13. South Africa
14. London Wasps
15. B) Rory Underwood (49)
16. False – it was South Africa's Brian Habana with eight tries
17. France (three times) and Wales (twice)
18. A) Le Crunch
19. C) England
20. Rob Andrew

Crossword (p.38)
1   SEVEN
2   SENTOFF
3   MURRAYFIELD
4   ROBANDREW
5   DROPKICK
6   CRYSTALPALACE
7   AILBLACKS
8   ANKLETAP
9   ELITESQUAD
10   SOUTHAFRICA
11   LONDONWASPS
12   BORTHWICK
13   SPRINGBOKS
14   JOHNNO
15   LINEOUT
16   SALESHARKS
17   NEWZEALAND
18   PARIS
19   WALLABIES
20   ALEX

Guess Who (p. 43)
1   Toby Flood
2   Paul Sackey
3   Danny Cipriani
4   Lesley Vainikolo